THE MONEY STORIES

UNDERSTANDING PERSONAL FINANCE WITH STORIES

YASWANTH SAI PALAGHAT

Copyright © Yaswanth Sai Palaghat
All Rights Reserved.

This book has been self-published with all reasonable efforts taken to make the material error-free by the author. No part of this book shall be used, reproduced in any manner whatsoever without written permission from the author, except in the case of brief quotations embodied in critical articles and reviews.

The Author of this book is solely responsible and liable for its content including but not limited to the views, representations, descriptions, statements, information, opinions and references ["Content"]. The Content of this book shall not constitute or be construed or deemed to reflect the opinion or expression of the Publisher or Editor. Neither the Publisher nor Editor endorse or approve the Content of this book or guarantee the reliability, accuracy or completeness of the Content published herein and do not make any representations or warranties of any kind, express or implied, including but not limited to the implied warranties of merchantability, fitness for a particular purpose. The Publisher and Editor shall not be liable whatsoever for any errors, omissions, whether such errors or omissions result from negligence, accident, or any other cause or claims for loss or damages of any kind, including without limitation, indirect or consequential loss or damage arising out of use, inability to use, or about the reliability, accuracy or sufficiency of the information contained in this book.

Made with ♥ on the Notion Press Platform
www.notionpress.com

To all of you who have followed my content on social media, thank you for your support and encouragement. Your belief in my work has been a source of inspiration and motivation for me, and I am grateful for the opportunity to share my ideas with you.

I would also like to thank all of you who supported my previous two books, "The Door To Financial Freedom" & "The Art Of Unleashing Your Potential". Your kind words and positive feedback were truly appreciated, and I hope that this book will provide even more value and guidance to you on your journey toward success and fulfillment.

Finally, I want to express my deep gratitude to all of the people who have helped me along the way, including my friends, family, colleagues, and mentors. Your support and guidance have been invaluable, and I am forever grateful for all that you have done for me.

With heartfelt thanks, Yaswanth Sai Palaghat

Contents

Contents

Contents

Foreword

Money management is a vital skill that we all need to learn, but unfortunately, it's not always taught in schools or homes. That's why I'm thrilled to introduce **"The Money Stories: Understanding Personal Finance With Stories"**, a book that offers a fresh and engaging approach to learning about money management.

As a finance content creator, I've seen firsthand how important it is for people to understand the basics of personal finance. That's why I believe "The Money Stories" is such an important resource. By sharing real-life stories and practical advice, this book provides readers with a solid foundation in money management, whether they're just starting out or looking to improve their financial skills.

What I love most about "The Money Stories" is how it makes learning about personal finance fun and accessible. By using stories to illustrate financial concepts, readers are able to connect with the material in a way that's relatable and engaging. Whether you're a student, a young adult, or just someone who wants to take control of your finances, this book is an invaluable resource that will help you achieve your financial goals.

I highly recommend "The Money Stories: Understanding Personal Finance With Stories" to anyone who wants to gain a better understanding of personal finance. With its practical advice, relatable stories, and engaging approach, this book is sure to help readers on their journey toward financial success.

Preface

Managing money can be overwhelming, especially for students and young adults who are just starting out. As a finance content creator I've seen the impact that a lack of financial knowledge can have on people's lives. That's why I wrote "The Money Stories: Understanding Personal Finance With Stories", a book that offers a fresh and engaging approach to learning about personal finance.

In this book, I share real-life stories that illustrate essential financial concepts, such as budgeting, saving, investing, and more. Each story is accompanied by practical advice and tips that readers can apply to their own lives. My goal is to help readers gain a deeper understanding of personal finance, and to empower them to take control of their financial futures.

"The Money Stories" is not your typical finance textbook. It's a collection of relatable stories that are designed to make learning about money management fun and accessible. Whether you're a student, a young adult, or just someone who wants to improve their financial skills, this book is for you.

I hope that "The Money Stories: Understanding Personal Finance With Stories" will help readers gain the confidence and knowledge they need to make smart financial decisions. Thank you for joining me on this journey towards financial freedom!

CHAPTER ONE

Introduction to Personal Finance: The Basics You Need to Know

Personal finance is all about managing your money in a smart way so that you can achieve your financial goals, both in the short-term and in the long-term. It is important to start learning about personal finance early in life so that you can make informed financial decisions and develop healthy money habits.

One of the most important things to understand about personal finance is budgeting. This means keeping track of how much money you earn and how much you spend each month. You can create a budget by writing down all of your income sources and your expenses, including things like rent, food, entertainment, and savings. It's important to make sure that your expenses don't exceed your income, and that you're putting money away into savings each month.

Another key aspect of personal finance is saving money. This means putting money aside for things you want or need in the future, like a new phone, a car, or college tuition. You should aim to save at least 10% of your income each month, and you can do this by setting up automatic transfers to a savings account. It's important to have both short-term and long-term savings goals, and to make a plan for how you will reach them.

When it comes to spending money, it's important to be mindful of your choices. It's easy to get tempted by impulse purchases or by what your friends are buying, but it's important to make sure that you're spending your money on things that truly matter to you. You should always try to find the best deals and avoid unnecessary expenses, like paying for subscription services that you don't use.

Finally, it's important to understand credit and debt. Credit is when you borrow money and promise to pay it back later, usually with interest. It's important to use credit responsibly and to only borrow what you can afford to pay back. Debt can be a major burden, so it's important to try to avoid it if possible.

In conclusion, personal finance is all about making smart decisions with your money. By creating a budget, saving money, spending wisely, and understanding credit and debt, you can achieve your financial goals and build a healthy financial future for yourself.

CHAPTER TWO

Goal Setting: How to Set Financial Goals and Achieve Them

Once upon a time, there was a young girl named Lily who loved to play the guitar. She dreamed of owning a beautiful electric guitar and joining a band with her friends.

One day, Lily's parents suggested that she start setting financial goals to save up for her dream guitar. They explained that by setting specific goals, Lily could work towards achieving her objective and learn valuable financial skills along the way.

Lily decided to set a goal of saving up $500 to buy her dream guitar. She created a plan to achieve her goal by putting aside a portion of her allowance or pocket money each week and doing extra chores around the house to earn extra money.

As she worked towards her goal, Lily learned about the importance of budgeting, saving, and delaying gratification. She realized that by prioritizing her savings and making small sacrifices along the way, she could achieve her financial objectives and buy her dream guitar.

After several months of saving, Lily was finally able to buy her dream guitar. She was proud of her accomplishment and knew that she had developed valuable financial skills that would benefit her throughout her life.

This story illustrates how goal setting can help young people achieve their financial objectives, whether it's saving up for a guitar, a video game console, or any other item they desire.

Here are some reasons why goal setting is important in life:

1. **Provides focus and direction:** When you set clear financial goals, you have a target to work towards. This gives you focus and direction, and helps you prioritize your spending and saving habits.
2. **Increases motivation:** Knowing what you want to achieve with your money can be a powerful motivator. When you have a specific goal in mind, you're more likely to stay committed to your financial plan and make the necessary sacrifices to achieve it.
3. **Helps measure progress:** By setting specific goals, you can track your progress and measure your success. This allows you to celebrate your achievements along the way and adjust your strategy if necessary.
4. **Encourages smart decision-making:** Setting financial goals requires careful planning and consideration. It forces you to think critically about your priorities and encourages you to make smart decisions with your money.
5. **Provides a sense of accomplishment:** Achieving financial goals can be incredibly rewarding. It gives you

a sense of accomplishment and provides a tangible outcome for all of your hard work and dedication.

In summary, goal setting is an essential aspect of personal finance. It provides focus, motivation, and direction for your financial decisions, and helps you measure progress and celebrate achievements along the way. By setting clear financial goals, you can create a roadmap for your financial future and build a solid foundation for your financial success.

CHAPTER THREE

Budgeting: Creating a Budget That Works for You

Once upon a time, there was a young girl named Maya who loved to read books. She would often visit the local bookstore and spend hours browsing through the shelves, looking for new titles to add to her collection.

One day, Maya's parents suggested that she start budgeting for her book purchases. They explained that by creating a budget and managing her money carefully, Maya could buy more books and still save money for other things she wanted.

Maya decided to create a budget that allocated a certain amount of money each month towards buying new books. She also set a goal to save a portion of her allowance each week towards her future college education.

As she tracked her expenses carefully, Maya learned about the importance of prioritizing her spending and making informed financial decisions. She discovered that by creating a budget and sticking to it, she could achieve her financial objectives and still enjoy her favorite hobby.

Over time, Maya was able to expand her book collection and save money for her future. She was proud of her accomplishments and knew that she had developed valuable financial skills that would benefit her throughout her life.

This story illustrates how budgeting can help young people manage their money effectively and achieve their financial goals. By creating a budget, prioritizing spending, and making informed financial decisions, kids can learn valuable financial skills and develop good financial habits that will benefit them throughout their lives.

Here are some reasons why budgeting is important:

1. **Helps you achieve your financial goals:** Budgeting allows you to allocate your money towards specific goals, such as saving for a down payment on a house or paying off debt. By creating a budget, you can prioritize your spending and make sure your money is going towards the things that matter most to you.
2. **Helps you plan for the future:** A budget helps you plan for the future by allowing you to set aside money for unexpected expenses and emergencies. By having a financial cushion, you can avoid going into debt or having to rely on credit cards when unexpected expenses arise.
3. **Helps you track your spending:** By tracking your spending, you can identify areas where you may be overspending and make adjustments to your budget. This can help you save money and stay within your financial means.

4. **Reduces stress and anxiety:** Financial stress and anxiety can take a toll on your mental health. By creating a budget and sticking to it, you can reduce financial stress and feel more in control of your money.
5. **Provides a sense of security:** Budgeting provides a sense of security by allowing you to live within your means and avoid overspending. This can give you peace of mind and help you feel more confident about your financial future.

In summary, budgeting is an important aspect of life as it allows you to manage your finances effectively and make informed decisions about how to spend your money. By creating a budget, you can prioritize your spending, plan for the future, track your spending, reduce stress and anxiety, and feel more secure about your financial future.

CHAPTER FOUR

Saving: Strategies for Saving Money and Building Wealth

Once upon a time, there was a young boy named Alex who loved to play video games. He would spend hours on end playing his favorite games, but he never thought much about saving his money.

One day, Alex's parents suggested that he start saving his money so he could buy even more games. They explained that by saving his money, he could afford to buy more games and also have money for other things he wanted in the future.

Alex decided to start saving his allowance by putting aside a small portion each week into a piggy bank. As he saw his savings grow, he felt a sense of accomplishment and began to think more about his financial future.

Over time, Alex learned about the importance of saving for emergencies, like unexpected car repairs or medical bills. He also discovered that saving could help him achieve bigger goals, like going on a trip or buying a car.

As he continued to save, Alex developed good financial habits that would benefit him throughout his life. He learned to live within his means, avoid unnecessary spending, and prioritize his financial goals.

This story illustrates how saving can help young people achieve their financial objectives and develop good financial habits. By starting small and putting aside money regularly, kids can learn the value of saving and prepare for their financial future.

Here are some reasons why saving is important:

1. **Provides financial security:** Saving money provides a financial cushion in case of unexpected events such as losing your job, medical emergencies, or unexpected home or car repairs. Having a savings account can help you avoid debt and provide peace of mind in case of unexpected expenses.
2. **Helps you achieve your long-term goals:** Whether it's buying a home, starting a business, or saving for retirement, saving money is crucial for achieving your long-term goals. By regularly contributing to a savings account, you can accumulate the money you need to achieve your goals.
3. **Enables you to take advantage of opportunities:** Saving money allows you to take advantage of opportunities that may arise in the future. For example, having a savings account can enable you to invest in a business or take advantage of a once-in-a-lifetime travel opportunity.

4. **Builds financial discipline:** Saving money requires discipline and self-control, which can translate to other areas of your life. Building financial discipline through saving can help you make better financial decisions in the future.
5. **Reduces financial stress:** Having savings can reduce financial stress and anxiety, allowing you to focus on other areas of your life. Knowing that you have money saved for emergencies and long-term goals can help you feel more secure about your financial future.

In summary, saving money is an essential aspect of personal finance that provides financial security, enables you to achieve your long-term goals, builds financial discipline, reduces financial stress, and allows you to take advantage of opportunities that may arise in the future. By making saving a priority, you can achieve financial stability and a brighter financial future.

CHAPTER FIVE

Debt: Understanding Debt and Managing it Effectively

Once upon a time, there was a young student named Max who wanted to buy a new video game console. He saved up his allowance for several months but still didn't have enough money to buy it. So, he decided to ask his parents for help.

His parents explained to him that they could either buy the console for him as a gift or they could lend him the money and he could pay them back over time. They also explained the concept of interest and how borrowing money could be expensive if he didn't pay it back on time.

Max decided to borrow the money from his parents and agreed to pay them back with a portion of his allowance each month. He learned the importance of managing his debts and paying them back on time.

This story illustrates how young people can learn about debt and borrowing money from their parents in a responsible and appropriate way. It's important to teach children about debt management and the consequences of not paying it back on time, so they can develop good financial habits for the future.

Here are some tips on how to manage and avoid debt:

1. **Create a budget:** One of the best ways to manage and avoid debt is to create a budget. A budget can help you keep track of your expenses and ensure that you are not spending more than you earn. By creating a budget, you can identify areas where you can cut back on spending and save more money.
2. **Prioritize debt repayment:** If you have debt, it's important to prioritize debt repayment. Make a list of your debts and focus on paying off high-interest debt first. By prioritizing debt repayment, you can reduce your debt faster and save money on interest charges.
3. **Use credit cards wisely:** Credit cards can be a useful tool for building credit and earning rewards, but they can also lead to debt if not used responsibly. To avoid credit card debt, only use credit cards for necessary expenses and pay off the balance in full each month.
4. **Avoid unnecessary debt:** Avoid taking on unnecessary debt, such as high-interest loans or credit card debt for non-essential purchases. Before taking on any debt, consider whether it is necessary and whether you can afford the monthly payments.
5. **Build an emergency fund:** Building an emergency fund can help you avoid debt in case of unexpected expenses or emergencies. Aim to save three to six months' worth of living expenses in an easily accessible savings account.

In summary, managing and avoiding debt is an important aspect of personal finance. By creating a budget, prioritizing debt repayment, using credit cards wisely, avoiding unnecessary debt, and building an emergency fund, you can manage debt and achieve financial stability. With these tips, you can take control of your finances and avoid the negative impact of debt on your financial future.

CHAPTER SIX

Credit: Building and Maintaining Good Credit

Once upon a time, there was a young student named Alex who was getting ready to graduate from high school. He wanted to apply for a student credit card to help him start building his credit score.

Before applying, Alex did some research and learned about credit scores and how they can affect his ability to borrow money in the future. He also learned that his credit score is based on his credit history, including things like whether he pays his bills on time, how much debt he has, and how long he has had credit.

Alex decided to start small and applied for a student credit card with a low credit limit. He made sure to use it responsibly by only charging what he could afford to pay back each month and paying his bills on time.

Over time, Alex's credit score improved, and he was able to qualify for higher credit limits and better interest rates on loans. He learned the importance of building good credit and using credit responsibly to achieve his financial goals.

This story illustrates the importance of understanding credit scores and how to build good credit from a young age. By teaching children about credit and responsible borrowing, they can develop good financial habits that will serve them well throughout their lives.

Here are some tips on how to build and maintain good credit:

1. **Understand how credit works:** To build and maintain good credit, it's important to understand how credit works. Credit is a measure of how likely you are to repay a debt based on your past credit history. Your credit score is a numerical representation of your creditworthiness and is used by lenders to determine whether to approve you for credit and at what interest rate.
2. **Pay your bills on time:** One of the most important factors in building and maintaining good credit is paying your bills on time. Late payments can negatively impact your credit score and make it harder to obtain credit in the future.
3. **Keep your credit utilization low:** Credit utilization is the amount of credit you are using compared to the amount of credit you have available. Keeping your credit utilization low can help improve your credit score. Aim to keep your credit utilization below 30% of your available credit.
4. **Monitor your credit report:** Regularly monitoring your credit report can help you identify errors and potential fraud. You are entitled to a free credit report from each of the three major credit bureaus every year. Review

your credit report for errors and report any discrepancies.

5. **Use credit responsibly:** Using credit responsibly is key to building and maintaining good credit. Only use credit for necessary expenses and make sure you can afford the monthly payments. Avoid maxing out your credit cards or applying for too much credit at once.

In summary, building and maintaining good credit is an important aspect of personal finance. By understanding how credit works, paying your bills on time, keeping your credit utilization low, monitoring your credit report, and using credit responsibly, you can build and maintain good credit and achieve financial stability. With these tips, you can take control of your finances and improve your creditworthiness.

CHAPTER SEVEN

Investing: Introduction to Investing and Building Wealth for the Future

Once upon a time, there was a young girl named Emma who received a gift of money from her grandparents for her birthday. Emma decided that instead of spending the money right away, she wanted to invest it to make it grow.

Emma did some research and learned about different types of investments, such as stocks, bonds, and mutual funds. She also learned about the concept of risk and return, which means that investments with higher potential returns also have higher potential risks.

Emma decided to start small by investing in a mutual fund that included a mix of stocks and bonds. She monitored her investment regularly and made adjustments as necessary.

Over time, Emma's investment grew, and she was able to use the money to pay for college tuition. She learned the importance of investing wisely and how it can help achieve long-term financial goals.

This story illustrates the importance of understanding investing and making informed decisions about where to put your money. By teaching children about investing, they can develop good financial habits and set themselves up for a secure financial future.

Investing is a powerful tool for building wealth and securing your financial future.

Here are some key things to consider when getting started with investing:

1. **Understand your goals:** Before you start investing, it's important to have a clear understanding of your financial goals. Are you looking to save for retirement, pay for a child's education, or save for a down payment on a home? Different goals may require different investment strategies.
2. **Know your risk tolerance:** Investing involves risk, and it's important to understand your own risk tolerance. How much risk are you comfortable taking on? Are you willing to invest in high-risk, high-reward investments or do you prefer a more conservative approach?
3. **Diversify your portfolio:** Diversification is key to building a strong investment portfolio. This means investing in a variety of asset classes, such as stocks, bonds, and real estate. Diversification can help reduce risk and improve returns over the long term.
4. **Start early:** The earlier you start investing, the more time you have to grow your investments. Even small amounts invested regularly can add up over time, thanks to the power of compounding.

5. **Keep fees low:** Fees can eat into your investment returns over time. Look for low-cost investment options, such as index funds, to help keep fees low.
6. **Stay informed:** Investing requires ongoing education and research. Keep up-to-date on market trends and news that could impact your investments. Consider working with a financial advisor to help guide your investment decisions.

By following these key principles, you can start building wealth for the future and achieve your financial goals. Remember, investing is a long-term game, and it's important to stay committed and patient over time. With a solid investment strategy in place, you can achieve financial success and secure your financial future.

CHAPTER EIGHT

Retirement Planning: Preparing for Your Golden Years

Samantha was always a hard worker. She had been working since she was 16 and had saved up some money over the years. But as she got older, she began to realize that she wasn't going to be able to work forever. So she started thinking about her retirement.

At first, Samantha wasn't sure where to start. Retirement planning seemed overwhelming and complicated. But she did some research and found out that it was actually pretty simple. She just needed to start saving money and investing it wisely.

Samantha started by creating a budget and figuring out how much money she could afford to save each month. She then opened a retirement account and began investing in low-cost index funds. She also looked into other ways to save money, such as downsizing her home and cutting back on unnecessary expenses.

It wasn't always easy, but Samantha stayed committed to her retirement plan. She watched her savings grow over time and felt a sense of peace knowing that she was preparing for her golden years.

When Samantha finally retired, she was able to enjoy her retirement without worrying about money. She traveled, pursued her hobbies, and spent time with loved ones. She was grateful that she had taken the time to plan for her retirement and felt secure in her financial future.

Retirement planning is an important part of your financial journey, and it's never too early (or too late!) to start thinking about it.

Here are some key things to consider when preparing for your golden years:

1. **Determine your retirement needs:** Think about what you want your retirement to look like. Do you want to travel? Pursue hobbies? Downsize your home? All of these things can impact how much money you'll need in retirement.
2. **Start saving early:** The earlier you start saving for retirement, the better. Compound interest can work wonders over time, so it's important to start building your retirement savings as soon as possible.
3. **Take advantage of retirement accounts:** Retirement accounts, such as 401(k)s and IRAs, offer tax advantages that can help your money grow more quickly. Take advantage of these accounts and consider contributing the maximum amount each year.
4. **Consider working with a financial advisor:** A financial advisor can help you create a retirement plan that's tailored to your needs and goals. They can also help you navigate complex retirement issues, such as Social

Security and Medicare.

5. **Plan for healthcare costs:** Healthcare costs can be a major expense in retirement. Make sure you have a plan in place to cover these costs, whether through Medicare, private insurance, or other means.
6. **Adjust your plan as needed:** Your retirement plan should be flexible and adaptable. As your life changes, your retirement needs and goals may change as well. Be prepared to adjust your plan as needed to stay on track.

By taking these steps, you can prepare for a comfortable and secure retirement. Remember, retirement planning is a long-term process that requires careful thought and planning. With a solid retirement plan in place, you can enjoy your golden years with confidence and peace of mind.

CHAPTER NINE

Taxes: Understanding Taxes and Maximizing Your Refund

Once upon a time, there was a boy named Max who loved earning money by selling lemonade on the street. But when it came time to pay taxes on his earnings, he didn't understand why he had to give some of his hard-earned money away.

His dad explained to him that taxes are a way for the government to fund important services, like schools and roads, that benefit everyone in the community. He also explained that there are ways to maximize your refund by keeping track of your expenses and deductions.

Max learned that he could deduct the cost of the lemons, sugar, and cups he used to make his lemonade, as well as any other expenses related to his business. He also learned that he could invest in a few mutual funds, to reduce his taxable income and potentially earn a tax credit.

With his new knowledge, Max was able to file his taxes confidently and even received a larger refund than he expected. He realized that paying taxes is an important part of being a responsible citizen and that understanding how they work can help you make the most of your money.

Here are some key things to consider when it comes to taxes:

1. **Know your tax bracket:** Your tax bracket determines the percentage of your income that goes towards taxes. Understanding your tax bracket can help you plan for tax payments and maximize your refund.
2. **Take advantage of deductions and credits:** Deductions and credits can help lower your tax bill and increase your refund. Be sure to take advantage of any deductions or credits you're eligible for, such as charitable donations or education expenses.
3. **Keep accurate records:** Keeping accurate records of your income and expenses can make tax season much easier. Make sure to keep all relevant documents, such as receipts and bank statements, organized and easily accessible.
4. **Consider hiring a professional:** If your taxes are particularly complex or you're not comfortable preparing them on your own, consider hiring a professional tax preparer. They can help ensure that you're taking advantage of all available deductions and credits, and help maximize your refund.
5. **Plan ahead:** Don't wait until tax season to start thinking about your taxes. Throughout the year, keep track of your income and expenses, and consider making estimated tax payments to avoid a large tax bill at the end of the year.

By understanding taxes and taking advantage of available deductions and credits, you can maximize your refund and minimize your tax bill. With careful planning and organization, tax season doesn't have to be a source of stress or anxiety.

CHAPTER TEN

Insurance: Protecting Your Assets and Managing Risk

Once upon a time, there was a family named the Smiths. They worked hard to build a comfortable life for themselves, but they knew that unexpected events could threaten their financial security. That's why they made sure to have insurance for their home, car, and health.

One day, Mr. Smith got into a car accident on his way to work. Thankfully, he wasn't hurt, but his car was badly damaged. He called his insurance company to file a claim and was relieved to find out that his policy covered the cost of repairs.

A few weeks later, Mrs. Smith had a medical emergency and had to be hospitalized. Again, they were grateful for their health insurance, which covered most of the medical expenses.

The Smiths realized that insurance was more than just a monthly bill; it was a way to protect their assets and manage risk. They made sure to review their policies regularly to make sure they had adequate coverage and to explore ways to lower their premiums, such as bundling policies or raising deductibles.

By understanding insurance and taking steps to protect their assets, the Smiths could rest easy knowing that they were prepared for whatever life might throw their way.

Here are some key things to consider when it comes to insurance:

1. **Understand your risks:** The first step in managing risk is to understand what you're trying to protect against. This might include risks related to your health, property, or business.
2. **Choose the right types of insurance:** There are many different types of insurance available, including health insurance, car insurance, home insurance, and business insurance. Each type of insurance is designed to protect against different types of risks, so it's important to choose the right policies for your needs.
3. **Shop around for the best rates:** Insurance premiums can vary widely between providers, so it's important to shop around and compare rates before making a purchase. Be sure to consider factors like deductibles, coverage limits, and exclusions when comparing policies.
4. **Understand your policy:** Once you've purchased insurance, it's important to understand the terms and conditions of your policy. Be sure to read the fine print and ask questions if anything is unclear.
5. **Re-evaluate your coverage regularly:** Your insurance needs may change over time, so it's important to re-evaluate your coverage regularly to ensure that you're

adequately protected.

Types of Insurance:

1. **Health Insurance:** Provides coverage for medical expenses, including doctor visits, hospitalizations, and prescription drugs.
2. **Vehicle Insurance:** Provides coverage for damage or injury resulting from vehicle accidents.
3. **Homeowners Insurance:** Provides coverage for damage or loss of your home and its contents due to fire, theft, or other covered events.
4. **Life Insurance:** Provides financial support to your loved ones in the event of your death.
5. **Disability Insurance:** Provides income replacement if you're unable to work due to illness or injury.
6. **Business Insurance:** Provides coverage for risks related to running a business, such as liability, property damage, and employee injuries.

By understanding your risks and choosing the right types of insurance, you can protect your assets and manage risk effectively. With careful consideration and planning, insurance can provide peace of mind and financial security.

CHAPTER ELEVEN

Financial Planning: The Importance of Creating a Financial Plan

Lena had just started her first job after graduating from college. She was excited to have a steady income and wanted to start spending on all the things she had been dreaming of. However, her father, who had always been wise with his finances, sat her down and gave her some advice.

"Listen, Lena," he said. "Now that you have a steady income, it's important to start thinking about your financial future. You need to create a financial plan to make sure you can achieve all your goals in life."

Lena was confused. She had never thought about a financial plan before. Her father explained that a financial plan is a roadmap for achieving financial goals. It helps in understanding one's current financial situation, defining financial goals, and creating a plan to achieve those goals.

Lena's father helped her create a budget and track her expenses. He also explained how important it is to save for emergencies and invest for the future. He emphasized that a financial plan is not just about saving money, but also about being smart with it.

After creating a financial plan, Lena realized how much she was overspending on things she didn't really need. She started cutting back on unnecessary expenses and instead focused on saving and investing. She also opened a retirement account and started contributing to it regularly.

Thanks to her father's advice and her financial plan, Lena was able to save enough money to go on her dream vacation and even put a down payment on her own apartment. She felt secure in her financial future and knew that she was on the right track to achieving her long-term financial goals.

Financial planning is the process of setting goals, assessing your financial situation, creating a plan to achieve those goals, and regularly monitoring your progress. It's an important process that helps you make informed decisions about your finances and achieve your financial goals.

Creating a financial plan helps you to identify your financial strengths and weaknesses and prioritize your financial goals. By understanding your income, expenses, assets, and liabilities, you can create a plan that aligns with your values, goals, and aspirations. This plan will help you to make smart decisions about saving, spending, investing, and managing debt.

A financial plan can also help you to prepare for unexpected events such as a job loss, illness, or other financial challenges. By having a plan in place, you can feel more confident and in control of your financial future.

It's important to regularly review and update your financial plan to ensure that it reflects your changing circumstances and goals. By doing so, you can make adjustments as needed and stay on track to achieve your financial objectives.

Overall, creating a financial plan is a crucial step toward achieving financial security and stability. It's never too early or too late to start planning for your financial future.

CHAPTER TWELVE

Emergency Fund: Why You Need One and How to Build It

Once upon a time, there was a girl named Lily who was very responsible with her money. She always saved a portion of her pocket money and had a piggy bank where she kept all her spare change. One day, Lily's family faced an unexpected emergency when their home was damaged in a storm. They had to pay for repairs, but they didn't have enough money saved up to cover the costs.

Lily felt upset that she couldn't help her family and realized the importance of having an emergency fund. She decided to start building one herself and learned that an emergency fund is a separate savings account specifically for unexpected expenses like medical bills, car repairs, or sudden job loss.

Lily made a plan to save a portion of her allowance every week until she had enough money to cover three months' worth of her family's expenses. She put the money in a separate savings account so it wouldn't get mixed up with her regular savings.

After a few months of saving, Lily had built up a good emergency fund. One day, her younger brother fell ill and had to be hospitalized. Lily's family had to pay for the medical bills, but they were able to cover the costs thanks to the emergency fund Lily had set up.

From that day on, Lily realized the importance of being financially prepared for unexpected events. She continued to add to her emergency fund and encouraged her family and friends to do the same.

An emergency fund is a savings account that you set up specifically to cover unexpected expenses or financial emergencies. It's important to have an emergency fund to protect yourself from unforeseen circumstances, such as a sudden job loss, medical emergency, or unexpected home repair.

Having an emergency fund provides you with a safety net, giving you the peace of mind that comes with knowing that you are financially prepared for the unexpected. Without an emergency fund, you may have to rely on high-interest credit cards, loans, or other forms of debt to cover unexpected expenses. This can lead to long-term financial stress and can make it difficult to achieve your financial goals.

To build an emergency fund, start by setting a goal for how much you want to save. It's generally recommended to have 3 to 6 months' worth of living expenses saved up in your emergency fund. Then, create a budget and start saving a small amount each month until you reach your goal.

Make sure to keep your emergency fund in a separate account from your regular savings or checking account, so that you're not tempted to dip into it for everyday expenses. Consider keeping your emergency fund in a high-yield savings account or a money market account, where it can earn interest and grow over time.

Remember, building an emergency fund is a key component of any strong financial plan. By setting aside money for unexpected expenses, you'll be better prepared to handle any financial challenges that come your way.

CHAPTER THIRTEEN

Living Within Your Means: Managing Your Expenses and Avoiding Debt

Once upon a time, there was a family of four who always seemed to be short on money. No matter how much they earned, they never seemed to have enough to cover all their expenses. They often found themselves using credit cards to pay for groceries or other necessities, which only made their financial situation worse.

One day, the father realized that they needed to make a change. He sat down with his wife and children and went over all their monthly expenses, including bills, groceries, entertainment, and other miscellaneous expenses. He also looked at their income and realized that they were spending more than they were earning.

Together, the family decided to make some changes. They cut back on eating out and started cooking at home more often. They canceled some of their subscription services and found free or low-cost alternatives for entertainment. They even downsized their home to reduce their monthly mortgage payment.

By making these changes, the family was able to live within their means and avoid going into debt. They no longer had to rely on credit cards to make ends meet and could even start saving for their future.

The father taught his children the importance of managing expenses and avoiding debt. He explained that living within your means is not about depriving yourself of the things you enjoy, but rather finding ways to enjoy them while still staying within your budget.

Thanks to their new habits and mindset, the family was able to achieve financial stability and peace of mind.

Living within your means is an important part of managing your personal finances. It means that you are spending less money than you earn, and not relying on credit cards or loans to make ends meet. By living within your means, you can avoid debt and achieve your financial goals.

To start living within your means, it's important to create a budget. A budget will help you track your income and expenses, and ensure that you are spending less than you earn. Begin by tracking your income and all of your expenses, including rent, utilities, groceries, transportation, entertainment, and other costs. Then, compare your income and expenses to see where you can make cuts and save money.

One of the keys to living within your means is to avoid unnecessary expenses. This means cutting back on non-essential purchases and focusing on your needs versus wants. Consider shopping for deals and discounts, and buying generic or store-brand products instead of name-brand items. Additionally, look for ways to reduce your monthly bills, such as by cutting cable or internet services or negotiating lower rates for utilities and insurance.

Living within your means can also mean finding ways to increase your income, such as by taking on a side job or selling items that you no longer need. By increasing your income and reducing your expenses, you can achieve a balanced budget and avoid debt.

Remember, living within your means is an important part of achieving your financial goals. It takes discipline and commitment, but the rewards are worth it in the end. By managing your expenses and avoiding debt, you can achieve financial freedom and peace of mind.

CHAPTER FOURTEEN

Entrepreneurship: Starting and Running a Successful Business

Once upon a time, there was a young girl named Ava who had a passion for baking. She loved experimenting with new recipes and sharing her delicious creations with her family and friends. One day, Ava decided to turn her passion into a business and start selling her baked goods.

Ava knew that starting a business was no easy feat, but she was determined to make her dream a reality. She began by doing some research on the baking industry and analyzing the competition in her local area. She also talked to her parents about the costs associated with starting a business, such as buying ingredients, renting a commercial kitchen, and marketing her products.

After careful consideration, Ava created a business plan that outlined her goals, target market, marketing strategies, and financial projections. She also applied for the necessary licenses and permits to operate her business legally.

To promote her business, Ava started by selling her baked goods at a local farmer's market. She also created social media pages and a website to showcase her products and connect with potential customers. As her business grew, Ava hired a few employees to help with baking and selling.

Ava faced some challenges along the way, such as keeping up with demand during peak seasons and managing her finances effectively. However, she learned from her mistakes and made adjustments to her business model to improve profitability and sustainability.

In the end, Ava's hard work and perseverance paid off. Her business became a local sensation, and she even landed some catering gigs for weddings and corporate events. She was able to turn her passion for baking into a successful and fulfilling career as an entrepreneur.

Entrepreneurship is the process of starting and running a business venture with the goal of making a profit. While starting a business can be challenging, it can also be very rewarding both financially and personally.

Here are some key steps to consider when starting and running a successful business:

1. **Identify a Need or Opportunity:** Start by identifying a need or opportunity in the market that your business can address. Conduct market research and gather data to help you make informed decisions.
2. **Develop a Business Plan:** A business plan outlines the goals, strategies, and financial projections of your business. It helps you stay focused and on track as you work towards your goals.
3. **Secure Funding:** Determine how much funding you will need to start and run your business. Consider loans,

grants, investors, or crowdfunding as potential sources of funding.

4. **Register Your Business:** Register your business with the appropriate government agencies and obtain any necessary licenses or permits.
5. **Build a Team:** Hire a team of talented individuals who can help you achieve your goals. Look for individuals who share your vision and have the skills and experience necessary to help your business grow.
6. **Market Your Business:** Develop a marketing strategy to promote your business and attract customers. Utilize social media, advertising, and other channels to reach your target audience.
7. **Manage Your Finances:** Manage your finances carefully and keep accurate records. Track your expenses and revenue, and make adjustments as necessary to ensure profitability.
8. **Adapt and Grow:** As your business grows, be prepared to adapt and make changes as needed. Stay informed about industry trends and be open to new opportunities.

Starting and running a successful business takes hard work and dedication, but it can also be a fulfilling and rewarding experience. By following these key steps, you can increase your chances of success and achieve your entrepreneurial dreams.

CHAPTER FIFTEEN

Real Estate: Understanding Real Estate Investing and Homeownership

Once upon a time, there was a man named John who dreamed of owning a home of his own. He worked hard every day, saving as much money as he could, but he felt like he was never getting any closer to his goal.

One day, John decided to attend a seminar on real estate investing. There, he learned about the benefits of owning property and how he could use it to build wealth over time. He also learned about different types of real estate investments, such as rental properties, fix-and-flip projects, and commercial real estate.

Excited by the possibilities, John decided to take the plunge and invest in a small rental property. He found a duplex that was in need of some repairs, but he could see its potential. He used some of his savings to buy the property and spent several months fixing it up.

Soon enough, John had his first tenants in the property and was earning rental income every month. He was able to use this income to pay down the mortgage on the property, while also putting some money aside for future repairs and maintenance.

Over time, John continued to invest in real estate, buying and selling properties as his knowledge and experience grew. He also used his rental income to save up for a down payment on his own home, which he eventually purchased with cash.

Thanks to his real estate investments, John was able to build wealth and achieve his dream of owning a home of his own. He continued to invest in real estate, enjoying the benefits of passive income and long-term appreciation.

The moral of the story? Real estate can be a powerful tool for building wealth and achieving financial goals, but it requires knowledge, hard work, and patience. With the right strategy and a commitment to long-term success, anyone can become a successful real estate investor.

Real estate can be a great investment opportunity and an important aspect of personal finance. Whether you are looking to invest in real estate or buy a home, understanding the basics of real estate investing and homeownership can help you make informed decisions and build long-term wealth.

Real estate investing involves buying and holding property with the goal of generating income or capital gains. Rental properties can provide a steady stream of rental income, while appreciation in property values can lead to capital gains when you sell. However, investing in real estate also comes with risks, such as property damage, vacancies, and fluctuations in the housing market.

Homeownership is another important aspect of real estate. Owning a home can provide stability, tax benefits, and the potential for long-term appreciation in value. However, it also comes with expenses, such as mortgage payments, property taxes, and maintenance costs.

When it comes to real estate investing and homeownership, it's important to do your research and make informed decisions. Consider your financial goals and resources, as well as the potential risks and rewards. Seek professional advice from a real estate agent, financial advisor, or attorney to help guide you through the process.

Overall, real estate can be a valuable component of a well-rounded financial plan. By understanding the basics of real estate investing and homeownership, you can make informed decisions and build long-term wealth.

CHAPTER SIXTEEN

Stocks and Bonds: Investing in the Stock Market and Fixed Income Securities

John had always been interested in investing but never knew where to start. He decided to do some research and learn more about the stock market and fixed-income securities like bonds.

He started by opening a brokerage account and investing in a diverse range of stocks and bonds. He knew that investing in a variety of companies and industries would help reduce risk and improve his chances of getting a good return on his investment.

John also made sure to keep his investment expenses low by investing in index funds and ETFs (exchange-traded funds) that had low fees.

Over time, John watched his investments grow and was able to make significant gains on his investments. He also reinvested his dividends, which helped his investments grow even faster.

Of course, there were ups and downs along the way, as the stock market is prone to volatility. But John was patient and knew that investing was a long-term game. He stayed the course and avoided making rash decisions based on short-term market movements.

Overall, investing in stocks and bonds helped John grow his wealth and achieve his financial goals. He was able to retire comfortably and enjoy the fruits of his labor thanks to his smart investment decisions.

Investing in the stock market and fixed-income securities, such as bonds, can be a great way to build wealth over time.

Here are some key things to consider when getting started:

1. **Understand the basics:** Before investing in stocks and bonds, it's important to have a basic understanding of how they work. Stocks represent ownership in a company, while bonds represent a debt owed by a company or government entity.
2. **Consider your risk tolerance:** As with any investment, stocks, and bonds involve risk. It's important to consider your own risk tolerance before investing. Are you comfortable taking on more risk for potentially higher returns, or do you prefer a more conservative approach?
3. **Diversify your portfolio:** Diversification is key to reducing risk when investing. This means investing in a variety of stocks and bonds across different industries and sectors. Diversification can help improve returns and reduce the impact of any one investment performing poorly.

4. **Choose your investments wisely:** There are many different types of stocks and bonds to choose from, each with its own level of risk and potential returns. Consider working with a financial advisor or doing your own research to choose investments that align with your financial goals and risk tolerance.
5. **Be patient:** Investing in stocks and bonds is a long-term game. It's important to be patient and not panic during market downturns. Over the long term, stocks and bonds have historically provided strong returns.

Overall, investing in the stock market and fixed-income securities can be a great way to build wealth over time. By understanding the basics, diversifying your portfolio, choosing your investments wisely, and being patient, you can achieve financial success through investing.

CHAPTER SEVENTEEN

Mutual Funds and ETFs: Understanding the Basics of Funds and Exchange-Traded Funds

amantha had always been interested in investing but didn't know where to start. She had heard about mutual funds and exchange-traded funds (ETFs) but wasn't exactly sure what they were or how they worked. So, she decided to do some research and learn more.

Samantha discovered that mutual funds and ETFs are both investment vehicles that pool money from multiple investors to purchase a diversified portfolio of stocks, bonds, or other assets. The main difference between the two is how they are traded.

Mutual funds are priced at the end of each trading day and can only be bought or sold at that price. ETFs, on the other hand, trade like stocks throughout the day and their prices can fluctuate.

Samantha also learned that mutual funds and ETFs can offer many benefits, such as diversification, professional management, and low investment minimums. Plus, they can provide exposure to a wide range of markets and asset classes that may be difficult for individual investors to access on their own.

However, Samantha also realized that mutual funds and ETFs come with some risks, including market fluctuations, fees, and taxes. So, she decided to do some more research on how to evaluate different funds and choose ones that aligned with her investment goals and risk tolerance.

After doing her due diligence, Samantha decided to invest in a mix of mutual funds and ETFs that provided exposure to different asset classes and markets. She regularly monitored her investments and made adjustments as needed to ensure they remained aligned with her financial goals.

Thanks to her research and careful planning, Samantha was able to successfully invest in mutual funds and ETFs and achieve her long-term financial goals.

Mutual funds and exchange-traded funds (ETFs) are investment vehicles that allow individuals to pool their money together to invest in a diversified portfolio of stocks, bonds, and other assets.

Mutual funds and ETFs are managed by professional investment managers who use their expertise to select a mix of assets that aligns with the fund's investment objective.

Investing in mutual funds or ETFs is a simple way to diversify your portfolio and spread your investment risk. Rather than investing in individual stocks, bonds, or other assets, you can invest in a diversified portfolio with just one investment.

Additionally, mutual funds and ETFs offer investors a low-cost option for investing. Because these funds are made up of a large number of investors, the cost of managing the fund is spread across all investors, making the expense ratio of these funds typically lower than if an individual investor were to try to replicate the same portfolio on their own.

It's important to understand the investment objective and strategy of the mutual fund or ETF you are considering before investing. Different funds have different investment objectives, which may range from conservative to aggressive, and different strategies for achieving those objectives.

Furthermore, it's important to pay attention to the fees associated with mutual funds and ETFs, including expense ratios, management fees, and transaction costs. These fees can have a significant impact on your investment returns over time.

Overall, mutual funds and ETFs can be a great way for individuals to invest in a diversified portfolio with lower costs and less effort than attempting to do so on their own. However, it's important to do your research and understand the risks and fees associated with any investment before committing your money.

CHAPTER EIGHTEEN

Diversification: How to Diversify Your Investments for Maximum Returns

Sophia had always been interested in investing and had read numerous books on the topic. However, she struggled to get started because she didn't know where to put her money.

One day, she stumbled upon the concept of diversification. She learned that by investing in a variety of different assets, she could spread out her risk and potentially achieve better returns over time.

Excited by this idea, Sophia began to research different types of investments that she could add to her portfolio. She started with stocks and bonds, but quickly realized that she needed more variety.

She decided to invest in mutual funds and exchange-traded funds (ETFs), which offered exposure to a variety of different assets. She also added real estate to her portfolio by investing in a real estate investment trust (REIT).

By diversifying her investments, Sophia was able to manage her risk and reduce the impact of any single investment on her portfolio. She also found that she was able to achieve more consistent returns over time.

Of course, diversification is not a guarantee of success, and Sophia still had to do her due diligence and research each investment thoroughly. But by diversifying her investments, she was able to build a stronger, more resilient portfolio that could withstand market volatility and deliver long-term returns.

Diversification is a crucial aspect of investing that helps minimize risks and maximize returns. Simply put, it means not putting all your eggs in one basket. By spreading your investments across various asset classes, industries, and geographies, you can reduce your exposure to any one type of investment and protect yourself against market volatility.

Diversification allows you to balance the potential rewards and risks of different investments. For example, while stocks can offer high returns, they can also be volatile and subject to sudden price fluctuations. In contrast, bonds are generally more stable but offer lower returns. By holding a mix of stocks and bonds, you can benefit from the growth potential of equities while also providing a cushion against market downturns.

There are various ways to diversify your portfolio, such as investing in different asset classes, including stocks, bonds, and cash equivalents. You can also diversify within each asset class by investing in different industries or sectors, such as technology, healthcare, or energy. Investing in different regions and countries can also help diversify your portfolio.

In addition to diversification, it's important to regularly review your investments and rebalance your portfolio as needed. This means adjusting your holdings to maintain your desired asset allocation and ensure that your investments continue to align with your goals and risk tolerance.

Overall, diversification is a powerful strategy for managing risk and optimizing returns. By spreading your investments across different asset classes, sectors, and regions, you can build a more resilient portfolio and increase your chances of long-term success.

CHAPTER NINETEEN

Asset Allocation: Balancing Risk and Return in Your Investment Portfolio

Asset allocation is the process of dividing your investment portfolio among different asset classes, such as stocks, bonds, and cash, to balance risk and return. It's an important aspect of investing that can have a significant impact on your long-term financial success.

To understand the concept of asset allocation, let's take the example of a 30-year-old investor named Jane. Jane wants to invest $50,000 in the stock market to achieve her long-term financial goals, which include saving for retirement and buying a home.

Jane knows that investing in stocks can provide higher returns over the long-term, but it also comes with higher risk. She also knows that investing all her money in one stock can be very risky, so she decides to diversify her portfolio by investing in a mix of stocks, bonds, and cash.

Jane starts by allocating 70% of her portfolio to stocks, which are considered higher-risk but have the potential for higher returns. She then allocates 20% of her portfolio to bonds, which are considered lower-risk but have a lower potential for returns. Finally, she allocates the remaining 10% of her portfolio to cash, which is considered the lowest-risk investment option.

Over time, Jane monitors her portfolio and adjusts her asset allocation as needed based on market conditions and her personal financial goals. For example, if the stock market experiences a downturn, she may adjust her asset allocation to reduce her exposure to stocks and increase her exposure to bonds and cash.

By carefully balancing her investment portfolio through asset allocation, Jane is able to achieve her long-term financial goals while managing risk and maximizing returns. It's an important lesson for all investors to remember: proper asset allocation is key to long-term financial success.

Asset allocation is an important aspect of managing your investment portfolio. It involves dividing your investments among different asset classes such as stocks, bonds, real estate, and cash in a way that balances risk and return.

The goal of asset allocation is to create a portfolio that maximizes returns while minimizing risk. By spreading your investments across different asset classes, you can reduce the impact of any one investment on your portfolio's overall performance. This helps to cushion against market volatility and reduce the risk of significant losses.

There are many different asset allocation strategies, each with its own benefits and drawbacks. Some investors prefer a more aggressive approach with a higher allocation to stocks, while others opt for a more conservative approach with a higher allocation to bonds and cash.

Your asset allocation strategy should be tailored to your individual financial goals, risk tolerance, and investment timeline. Regularly reviewing and adjusting your portfolio's asset allocation can help ensure that it remains aligned with your objectives and financial situation. A financial advisor can assist you in determining the best asset allocation strategy for your specific needs.

CHAPTER TWENTY

Behavioral Finance: Understanding the Psychology of Money Management

Sarah was always a smart saver. She had a budget for every aspect of her life, and she knew exactly how much she could spend on groceries, entertainment, and other expenses each month. She had a savings account that she diligently contributed to, and she had even started investing in the stock market.

However, Sarah still found herself making impulsive purchases from time to time. She would sometimes splurge on clothes, shoes, and other unnecessary items, even if they were outside her budget. She knew this behavior wasn't sustainable in the long run, and she wanted to get better at managing her money.

That's when Sarah discovered the field of behavioral finance. She started reading books and articles about the psychology of money management, and she realized that her impulsive spending was driven by emotions and cognitive biases. She learned that people are wired to prioritize immediate gratification over long-term goals, which can lead to poor financial decisions.

Sarah decided to take action to overcome her biases and improve her financial decision-making. She set up automatic contributions to her investment accounts so that she wouldn't be tempted to skip a month or withdraw money early. She also started using a budgeting app that helped her track her expenses and visualize her progress toward her goals.

Over time, Sarah's efforts paid off. She became more disciplined in her spending habits and started making better investment decisions. She was able to achieve her financial goals faster than she ever thought possible, all thanks to the insights she gained from behavioral finance.

Sarah's experience is a testament to the power of understanding the psychology of money management. By recognizing our cognitive biases and emotions, we can make better financial decisions and achieve our long-term goals.

Behavioral finance is a field that combines finance and psychology to explain why people make irrational financial decisions. By understanding the psychology behind money management, individuals can become better investors and make smarter financial decisions.

One of the key principles of behavioral finance is the idea that emotions play a significant role in financial decision-making. People often make decisions based on their emotions, rather than relying on logic and reason. This can lead to impulsive investment decisions and a lack of proper planning.

Another important aspect of behavioral finance is the concept of cognitive biases. These biases are mental shortcuts that individuals use to simplify complex decisions, but they can also lead to flawed decision-making. Common cognitive biases include overconfidence, confirmation bias, and anchoring.

To overcome these biases and make better financial decisions, individuals can take steps such as creating a financial plan, sticking to a budget, and seeking the advice of a financial advisor. It's also important to understand one's own risk tolerance and investment goals.

By understanding the principles of behavioral finance, individuals can make more informed decisions and better manage their finances for the long term.

CHAPTER TWENTY-ONE

Opportunity Cost: How to Make Better Financial Decisions

Once upon a time, there was a young woman named Emily who had just graduated from college and landed her first job. She was excited to start earning money and managing her finances on her own.

One day, Emily received a bonus at work and decided to use the extra money to buy a new pair of shoes that she had been eyeing for a while. She felt great about her purchase and couldn't wait to wear them to work.

However, a few days later, Emily was invited to attend a networking event after work. She realized that the shoes she had just bought weren't suitable for the event and she would need to buy a new outfit to go with them.

Emily was challenged with a decision: should she spend more money on a new outfit, or wear something she already owned? She realized that if she bought a new outfit, she would be sacrificing the opportunity to use that money for something else, like investing it or saving it for a future purchase.

After considering her options, Emily decided to wear something she already owned and save the money for something more meaningful in the future. She realized that every financial decision comes with an opportunity cost, and she didn't want to sacrifice her future financial goals for a short-term purchase.

From then on, Emily started to make more intentional financial decisions and always considered the opportunity cost before making a purchase. She learned that by being mindful of her spending and investing her money wisely, she could make better financial decisions and reach her goals faster.

Opportunity cost is a key concept in financial decision-making. It refers to the cost of forgoing one option in favor of another. Every decision has an opportunity cost, whether it's investing money in one stock instead of another, or spending time on one project instead of another. Understanding opportunity cost can help you make better financial decisions.

For example, let's say you have $1,000 to invest. You're trying to decide between investing in Stock A, which has the potential to generate high returns, and Stock B, which is more stable but has lower potential returns. If you invest in Stock A, the opportunity cost is the potential returns you could have earned if you had invested in Stock B instead. On the other hand, if you invest in Stock B, the opportunity cost is the potential returns you could have earned if you had invested in Stock A instead.

Opportunity cost also applies to non-financial decisions. For example, if you decide to spend your time on one project, the opportunity cost is the potential benefits you could have gained from working on a different project instead.

Understanding opportunity cost can help you make better financial decisions by weighing the potential benefits and drawbacks of each option. It can also help you prioritize your goals and determine which decisions are most important to achieving them. By considering the opportunity cost of each decision, you can make more informed choices that will help you achieve your financial goals in the long run.

CHAPTER TWENTY-TWO

Time Value of Money: Understanding the Concept of Present Value and Future Value

Once upon a time, there were two friends, Jack and Jill. Jack had just received a $10,000 inheritance from his grandparents and was trying to decide what to do with the money. Jill suggested he invest the money in the stock market, but Jack was hesitant.

Jill explained the concept of time value of money to Jack. She told him that by investing his money now, he could earn a return on his investment over time. She also explained that the value of money changes over time due to inflation and the opportunity cost of not investing.

To help Jack understand, Jill used an example. She said, "Imagine you have $100 today and you can either spend it or invest it. If you decide to spend it, you won't have any money left tomorrow. But if you invest it, you could earn a return and have more than $100 tomorrow. So, the choice you make today affects what you'll have tomorrow."

Jack began to understand the concept and decided to invest his $10,000 in a low-cost index fund. Over the next 10 years, he earned an average annual return of 8%. Thanks to the power of compounding, his initial investment had grown to over $21,000.

Jill was pleased with Jack's success and said, "By understanding the time value of money, you were able to make a smart financial decision and turn your inheritance into a valuable asset."

From that day on, Jack became a believer in the importance of investing early and regularly to take advantage of the time value of money.

The time value of money is an essential concept in finance that highlights how the value of money changes over time. Essentially, money today is worth more than the same amount of money in the future due to the potential earning power of the funds. This concept is particularly important for making investment decisions and understanding the cost of borrowing.

For example, let's say you have the option to receive $1,000 today or in one year. If you choose to receive the money in one year, you are giving up the opportunity to earn interest on that money for a year. Assuming a 5% interest rate, the present value of $1,000 one year from now would be $952.38. This means that the $1,000 received today is worth more than the $1,000 received in one year.

The time value of money also plays a crucial role in calculating the future value of investments. By understanding how interest compounds over time, investors can make informed decisions about the potential growth of their investments. For instance, if you invest $1,000 today at a 5% interest rate, the future value of that investment after one year would be $1,050. Over time, this compounding effect can significantly increase the value of an investment.

By understanding the time value of money, individuals can make better financial decisions and evaluate the potential costs and benefits of different financial opportunities. Whether saving for retirement or considering a loan, the time value of money is a critical component of any financial decision-making process.

CHAPTER TWENTY-THREE

Compound Interest: The Power of Compounding and How to Make It Work for You

Once upon a time, there were two friends named Tom and Jerry. They both started their careers at the same time and earned the same salary. However, they had different approaches to managing their money.

Tom liked to spend his money as soon as he got his paycheck. He would buy new gadgets, go on expensive trips, and dine out at fancy restaurants. On the other hand, Jerry was more financially savvy. He saved a portion of his salary every month and invested it in a mutual fund that gave him a 7% annual return.

Tom used to mock Jerry for being stingy and not enjoying his life. But as time passed, Jerry's savings grew, and he started earning more from the compound interest on his investments. On the other hand, Tom struggled to pay his bills and had to work overtime to make ends meet.

One day, Jerry invited Tom over to his house and showed him his investment portfolio. Tom was surprised to see how much Jerry had saved and the returns he had earned from compound interest. Jerry explained to Tom how compound interest works, and how he was able to grow his savings over time by reinvesting the interest earned.

Tom realized that he had been missing out on the power of compounding and regretted not following Jerry's example earlier. He decided to start saving and investing his money wisely, so that he could also benefit from the power of compounding.

In the end, Tom and Jerry both learned an important lesson: the power of compound interest can help you grow your wealth over time, and it's never too late to start investing in your future.

Compound interest is a powerful tool in the world of finance. It's the concept of earning interest not only on the initial amount invested but also on the accumulated interest over time. This can lead to exponential growth over the long term, and it's a key component in building wealth.

Let's take an example. Say you invest $10,000 in a savings account that earns an annual interest rate of 5%. After one year, your investment will have grown to $10,500. But if you leave that money in the account for another year, you won't just earn 5% on the initial $10,000 - you'll earn 5% on the full $10,500. That means your investment will grow to $11,025 after two years.

If you continue to leave the money in the account, it will keep compounding over time. After ten years, your investment will have grown to $16,386. And after 30 years, it will be worth $43,219 - more than four times your initial investment!

The power of compounding is especially evident when investing for long-term goals, such as retirement. By starting early and letting your investments compound over decades, you can build a substantial nest egg.

But there's a catch. While compound interest can work wonders for your investments, it can also work against you when it comes to debt. Credit card debt, for example, typically compounds at high-interest rates, making it much more difficult to pay off over time.

So, the key takeaway is to take advantage of compound interest by investing early and consistently, while avoiding high-interest debt whenever possible. By doing so, you can harness the power of compounding and put it to work for your financial future.

CHAPTER TWENTY-FOUR

Inflation: Understanding Inflation and Its Impact on Your Money

Once upon a time, there was a small town where a loaf of bread cost just 50 cents. The townspeople were happy and content, as their money could buy them plenty of bread and other goods.

However, over time, the cost of producing the bread began to rise. The wheat that was used to make the bread became more expensive, and the baker had to pay his employees more to keep up with the rising cost of living.

As a result, the baker had to increase the price of his bread to $1.00 per loaf. At first, the townspeople were surprised and upset by the sudden increase, as they were used to paying just 50 cents. But as they began to understand the reasons behind the price increase, they realized that it was due to inflation.

Inflation is the rate at which the general level of prices for goods and services is rising. It's a natural part of the economy, and it can have a big impact on your money over time. As prices rise, the purchasing power of your money decreases, meaning that you can buy less with the same amount of money.

The townspeople began to adjust their spending habits, looking for ways to save money and make their dollars stretch further. Some started buying bread in bulk to save money, while others started growing their own wheat and making their own bread.

By adapting to the changing economic conditions, the townspeople were able to weather the effects of inflation and continue living their lives. And while the cost of bread may have gone up, they realized that they could still find ways to make their money work for them and achieve their financial goals.

Inflation is a phenomenon that affects the value of money and the purchasing power of individuals. Simply put, inflation refers to the rate at which the general price level of goods and services in an economy is increasing over time. While some inflation can be healthy for an economy, too much inflation can be detrimental to the value of money.

For example, let's say you have $100 in your bank account. If the inflation rate is 2%, then the cost of goods and services will increase by 2% over the next year. This means that the purchasing power of your $100 will be reduced by 2%. In other words, the same amount of money will be able to buy fewer goods and services in the future than it can today.

This is why it's important to factor inflation into your financial planning. If you're saving for a long-term goal, such as retirement, it's important to consider how inflation will impact the value of your savings over time. You may need to adjust your savings goals or investment strategies to account for inflation.

One way to protect your money from inflation is to invest in assets that have historically provided a hedge against inflation, such as real estate, commodities, or stocks. These assets have the potential to increase in value over time, which can help offset the effects of inflation on the value of your money.

In summary, understanding inflation and its impact on your money is an important part of financial literacy. By factoring inflation into your financial planning and investing in assets that have historically provided a hedge against inflation, you can help protect the value of your money and achieve your long-term financial goals.

CHAPTER TWENTY-FIVE

Currency Exchange: The Basics of Foreign Exchange Markets and Trading

John had been planning a trip to Europe for months. He had saved up enough money to cover his travel expenses, but he was worried about exchanging his dollars for euros.

He knew that the exchange rate could fluctuate and he didn't want to end up losing money. So, he did his research and learned about the basics of foreign exchange markets and trading.

John discovered that the exchange rate is the value of one currency compared to another currency. He also learned that the exchange rate is influenced by many factors, such as economic conditions, political stability, and central bank policies.

To get the best exchange rate possible, John decided to wait until he arrived in Europe to exchange his dollars for euros. He knew that currency exchange booths at airports and hotels typically charge higher fees and offer less favorable exchange rates.

When John arrived in Europe, he found a reputable currency exchange office in a central location. He was pleasantly surprised to find that the exchange rate was favorable, meaning he would receive more euros for his dollars than he had expected.

John exchanged his money and was pleased with the outcome. He had saved money by waiting to exchange his currency until he arrived in Europe and by choosing a reputable exchange office with a good exchange rate.

From that point on, John made sure to do his research before traveling to a foreign country to ensure that he was getting the best exchange rate possible. He knew that by being informed and taking the time to find a good exchange office, he could save money and get the most out of his travels.

Currency exchange, also known as forex or FX trading, is the act of buying and selling currencies with the goal of making a profit. Forex trading is done in the foreign exchange market, which is a global, decentralized marketplace where currencies are traded 24 hours a day, five days a week.

The foreign exchange market is the largest financial market in the world, with an average daily trading volume of over $5 trillion. It's an attractive market for traders because of its high liquidity and the ability to leverage trades, which can amplify potential profits.

However, currency exchange can also be highly volatile and risky. Exchange rates can fluctuate rapidly due to a variety of factors, such as changes in economic policy, geopolitical events, and global economic conditions.

To be successful in currency exchange, traders must understand the basics of foreign exchange markets and trading. This includes knowledge of exchange rates, currency pairs, and technical analysis, as well as an understanding of global economic conditions and news events that could impact currency values.

Many traders use technical indicators and trading algorithms to analyze market trends and make informed trading decisions. Risk management is also critical in forex trading, as traders must have a plan in place to limit potential losses.

Overall, currency exchange can be a lucrative market for skilled traders, but it's important to approach it with caution and a solid understanding of the fundamentals.

CHAPTER TWENTY-SIX

Financial Statements: Understanding Financial Statements and Their Importance

Emily had always been interested in business, but she didn't know much about finance. When she started her own company, she quickly realized that understanding financial statements was crucial to her success.

At first, Emily found the different financial statements confusing. There were income statements, balance sheets, and cash flow statements - each with their own set of numbers and jargon. But with some research and help from her accountant, Emily began to understand what each statement meant and how they worked together.

One day, Emily was meeting with a potential investor who asked to see her company's financial statements. Emily confidently handed over the documents, and as she walked through the numbers with the investor, she realized just how much she had learned. She was able to explain her company's revenue streams, expenses, and cash flow projections in detail.

Impressed by Emily's knowledge and organization, the investor agreed to fund her company. Emily felt proud and grateful for her hard work and dedication to learning about financial statements.

As her company grew, Emily continued to review her financial statements regularly. She used them to make strategic decisions about her business, such as when to hire more staff or invest in new equipment. By understanding her financial statements, Emily was able to run a successful and profitable business.

Financial statements are a crucial tool for understanding the financial health and performance of a business. They provide a snapshot of the company's financial position, performance, and cash flow over a specific period of time.

For example, let's say you're an investor considering buying stock in a company. Before making a decision, you would likely want to review the company's financial statements to assess its financial health and performance.

The most common financial statements are the balance sheet, income statement, and cash flow statement. The balance sheet provides an overview of the company's assets, liabilities, and equity at a specific point in time. The income statement shows the company's revenue, expenses, and net income over a specific period of time. The cash flow statement shows the inflows and outflows of cash over a specific period of time.

By reviewing these financial statements, you can gain insights into the company's financial position and make more informed investment decisions. For example, if a company has a lot of debt and limited cash flow, it may be at a higher risk of financial distress. Conversely, if a company has a strong balance sheet and steady cash flow, it may be a more attractive investment opportunity.

In addition to investors, financial statements are also important for businesses themselves. By regularly reviewing their financial statements, businesses can identify areas for improvement, track progress toward financial goals, and make strategic decisions about investments and operations.

In summary, financial statements are a critical tool for understanding the financial health and performance of a business. Whether you're an investor or a business owner, it's important to understand how to read and interpret financial statements in order to make informed financial decisions.

CHAPTER TWENTY-SEVEN

Financial Ratios: Analyzing Financial Ratios and Their Significance

Once upon a time, there was a small business owner named Sarah who ran a bakery. Sarah had always been passionate about baking and decided to turn her hobby into a business. However, she soon realized that running a business was more than just baking delicious treats.

Sarah was struggling to understand the financial health of her business. She knew she was making sales and had cash coming in, but she wasn't sure if she was profitable or not. She decided to seek help from a financial advisor.

The financial advisor taught Sarah about financial ratios and how they can be used to evaluate the financial health of a business. Sarah learned that financial ratios are important indicators of a company's performance and can help identify areas for improvement.

The advisor showed Sarah how to calculate and analyze different ratios, such as liquidity ratios, profitability ratios, and efficiency ratios. They looked at Sarah's balance sheet and income statement to calculate the ratios and analyze her business's financial health.

Through this process, Sarah realized that her business had a low profitability ratio, which indicated that she needed to increase her prices or decrease her expenses. She also discovered that her inventory turnover ratio was lower than the industry average, which meant that she needed to better manage her inventory to improve her cash flow.

Armed with this new knowledge, Sarah was able to make changes to her business and improve her financial health. She raised her prices, implemented better inventory management systems, and focused on controlling her expenses. Over time, her financial ratios improved, and her business became more profitable.

Thanks to the financial ratios, Sarah was able to gain a better understanding of her business's financial health and make informed decisions to improve it. She continued to monitor her ratios regularly, ensuring that her business remained healthy and profitable.

Financial ratios are an essential tool for analyzing a company's financial health. They provide insights into a company's liquidity, profitability, efficiency, and solvency.

Here are some key financial ratios to know:

1. **Current Ratio:** This ratio measures a company's ability to pay its short-term obligations with its current assets. A higher current ratio indicates that a company has a strong liquidity position.
2. **Debt-to-Equity Ratio:** This ratio measures the amount of debt a company has relative to its equity. A high

debt-to-equity ratio indicates that a company is heavily reliant on debt financing, which can increase financial risk.

3. **Gross Profit Margin:** This ratio measures the percentage of sales that remain after deducting the cost of goods sold. A higher gross profit margin indicates that a company is effectively managing its production costs.
4. **Return on Equity (ROE):** This ratio measures a company's ability to generate profit from its shareholders' investments. A higher ROE indicates that a company is generating more profit per dollar of equity.
5. **Price-to-Earnings Ratio (P/E Ratio):** This ratio measures a company's stock price relative to its earnings per share. A higher P/E ratio indicates that investors are willing to pay more for each dollar of earnings.

Understanding these financial ratios and how to analyze them can help investors make informed decisions about whether to buy, sell, or hold a company's stock. It can also help companies identify areas for improvement in their financial performance.

CHAPTER TWENTY-EIGHT

Cash Flow Management: Managing Your Cash Flow for Better Financial Health

Anna was a young entrepreneur who had recently started her own fashion boutique. She was excited about her new venture and had invested a lot of money in inventory, marketing, and setting up her store. However, after a few months, she started to notice that her cash flow was not looking good.

Anna realized that she had not been keeping track of her cash flow properly. She had been spending more than she was earning and had been relying on her savings to cover her expenses. As a result, she was running out of cash, and her business was struggling.

To address this issue, Anna decided to take a closer look at her cash flow. She began to track her inflows and outflows carefully, identifying areas where she could cut costs and improve her revenue streams. She also started to negotiate better payment terms with her suppliers and began to offer discounts to customers who paid in cash.

As a result of these changes, Anna was able to turn her cash flow around. She started to generate more revenue and was able to reduce her expenses. Her business became more profitable, and she was able to pay herself a salary for the first time.

Anna's experience highlights the importance of cash flow management. By keeping track of her cash flow and making strategic changes, she was able to improve her financial position and ensure the success of her business. Effective cash flow management is essential for anyone who wants to achieve financial stability and success.

Managing your cash flow is essential for achieving better financial health. It refers to the way money flows in and out of your bank account, including income, expenses, and savings. Effective cash flow management involves creating a budget, tracking your spending, and making informed financial decisions.

Creating a budget is the first step in managing your cash flow. This involves determining your income and expenses and allocating your money accordingly. It's important to prioritize your spending based on your needs and goals, and to avoid overspending on unnecessary items.

Tracking your spending is another key aspect of cash flow management. This means keeping track of all your expenses and identifying areas where you can cut back. By analyzing your spending habits, you can make adjustments to your budget and find ways to save money.

Making informed financial decisions is also critical to managing your cash flow. This means carefully evaluating the costs and benefits of different financial options, such as investment opportunities, loans, and credit cards. It's important to consider the impact of these decisions on your overall financial health and to avoid taking on more debt than you can handle.

By effectively managing your cash flow, you can improve your financial health, build wealth, and achieve your financial goals. It takes discipline and commitment, but the benefits are well worth it. With the right approach and a bit of hard work, anyone can achieve financial stability and success.

CHAPTER TWENTY-NINE

Estate Planning: Preparing Your Estate for Your Loved Ones

Once upon a time, there was a wealthy businessman named John who had accumulated a significant amount of wealth over the years. However, he had not taken any steps to plan for his estate and what would happen to his assets in the event of his untimely death.

One day, John was involved in a terrible car accident that left him hospitalized for several weeks. During this time, he realized the importance of estate planning and ensuring that his assets would be distributed according to his wishes.

After he recovered from his injuries, John immediately began working with an estate planning attorney to create a comprehensive estate plan. He made a list of all his assets, including his properties, investments, and business interests. He also considered his family's needs and how his assets could be used to provide for them in the future.

John decided to create a trust to manage his assets and distribute them to his loved ones according to his wishes. He appointed a trustee who would be responsible for managing the trust and ensuring that his wishes were carried out. He also created a will, which detailed how he wanted his personal assets to be distributed.

In addition to the trust and will, John also established powers of attorney and healthcare directives to ensure that his financial and medical affairs would be managed appropriately if he became incapacitated.

With his estate plan in place, John had peace of mind knowing that his assets would be distributed according to his wishes and that his loved ones would be taken care of after his passing. He also knew that he had taken steps to minimize the tax implications of his estate and avoid any potential disputes among his heirs.

In the end, John's estate plan was a testament to his foresight and dedication to ensuring that his family's future was secure, even after he was gone.

Estate planning is the process of making arrangements for the transfer of your assets to your heirs or beneficiaries after you pass away. It involves creating a comprehensive plan that covers all aspects of your estate, including your property, investments, and any other valuable assets.

The main objective of estate planning is to ensure that your assets are distributed according to your wishes and that your loved ones are provided for after you're gone. Estate planning can also help to minimize estate taxes, avoid probate, and protect your assets from creditors.

There are several important steps involved in estate planning. The first step is to create a will, which is a legal document that outlines your wishes regarding the distribution of your assets after you pass away. In your will, you'll name an executor, who is responsible for carrying out your wishes. It's important to choose someone you trust and who is capable of handling the responsibilities of being an executor.

Another important aspect of estate planning is determining who will receive your assets. This can be done by naming beneficiaries for your bank accounts, retirement plans, and life insurance policies. You can also create a trust to transfer your assets to your beneficiaries over time and to protect your assets from creditors.

Estate planning also involves taking steps to minimize estate taxes. This can include making gifts to your beneficiaries while you're still alive, establishing trusts, and using other tax planning strategies.

It's important to review and update your estate plan regularly to ensure that it reflects any changes in your life circumstances or wishes. For example, if you get married, divorced, or have children, you may need to update your will or beneficiaries.

In summary, estate planning is a crucial part of financial planning. By taking the time to create a comprehensive estate plan, you can ensure that your loved ones are provided for after you're gone, minimize estate taxes, and protect your assets.

CHAPTER THIRTY

Philanthropy: Giving Back and Making a Positive Impact on Society

Once upon a time, there was a successful businessman named John. He had a great job, a big house, and a loving family. Despite his success, John felt like he was missing something in life. He had always felt a desire to give back to the community and help others in need.

One day, John attended a charity event and was moved by the stories of those in need. He realized that he had the resources to make a difference and decided to start giving back. He started by making small donations to local charities and volunteering his time at homeless shelters and food banks.

As he became more involved, John decided to create his own foundation to focus on causes he was passionate about. He started by making a list of the issues that he felt were most important, such as education, healthcare, and the environment. He then researched organizations that were making a real impact in these areas and began making larger donations.

Over time, John's foundation grew, and he was able to make a significant difference in the lives of many people. He also found that giving back gave him a sense of purpose and fulfillment that he had never experienced before. He realized that while making money and achieving success was important, helping others was equally important and gave him a sense of meaning that he could not find anywhere else.

John's example inspired others in his community to give back, and together they were able to make a significant impact on the world around them. They proved that even small contributions can make a big difference, and that giving back can be one of the most rewarding experiences in life.

Philanthropy is the act of giving to charity and doing good for others. It's a noble cause that has the power to make a positive impact on society. Philanthropy can take many forms, from donating money to a charitable organization, volunteering time and skills, or simply spreading awareness about important issues.

One individual who understood the importance of philanthropy was John D. Rockefeller. He was one of the wealthiest men in the world, but he also believed in giving back to society. In fact, he donated more than $500 million during his lifetime to various causes, including education, medical research, and the arts.

Rockefeller's philanthropic efforts began in the late 19th century when he founded the Rockefeller Foundation. The foundation's mission was to promote the well-being of humanity throughout the world. Over the years, it has funded numerous projects, including the eradication of diseases like yellow fever and hookworm, as well as support for education and the arts.

In addition to the Rockefeller Foundation, Rockefeller also donated to other charities, including churches, hospitals, and universities. One notable donation was to the University of Chicago, where he provided funding for the establishment of the university's School of Social Service Administration. This school has since become one of the top social work programs in the United States.

Rockefeller's philanthropy had a profound impact on society. His contributions helped to improve healthcare, education, and the arts, among other areas. His legacy continues today, as many of the organizations he supported continue to make a difference in people's lives.

Philanthropy is not just for the wealthy, however. Anyone can make a difference through charitable giving and volunteer work. Whether it's donating to a local food bank, volunteering at a homeless shelter, or supporting a cause that is important to you, there are many ways to give back and make a positive impact on society.

Conclusion

Congratulations on completing this comprehensive guide to personal finance! We hope that you have gained valuable insights and practical tips on how to manage your money wisely and achieve your financial goals.

Throughout this book, I have covered 30 essential topics that every individual should know to make informed financial decisions. From budgeting and saving to investing and retirement planning, I have provided you with a solid foundation in personal finance.

By understanding the concepts of time value of money, compound interest, inflation, and risk management, you can make better financial decisions that maximize your returns and minimize your risks. Furthermore, by learning about the importance of financial planning, estate planning, and philanthropy, you can create a legacy that positively impacts your loved ones and society.

I hope that you take the knowledge gained from this book and use it to improve your financial well-being. Remember, personal finance is not a one-time task but a lifelong journey of learning and adapting. By staying informed, disciplined, and focused on your goals, you can achieve financial freedom and live the life you want.

Thank you for reading and best of luck on your financial journey!

9 798889 868194

Printed by Libri Plureos GmbH in Hamburg,
Germany